DE:CODE

LEARN THE LANGUAGE OF

SOCIAL MEDIA

BY WILLIAM ANTHONY

BookLife
PUBLISHING

©2019
BookLife Publishing Ltd.
King's Lynn
Norfolk, PE30 4LS

All rights reserved.
Printed in Malaysia.

A catalogue record for this book is available from the British Library.

ISBN: 978-1-78637-694-7

Written by:
William Anthony

Edited by:
Madeline Tyler

Designed by:
Dan Scase

All facts, statistics, web addresses and URLs in this book were verified as valid and accurate at time of writing.

No responsibility for any changes to external websites or references can be accepted by either the author or publisher.

HOW TO DE:CODE THE LANGUAGE OF SOCIAL MEDIA

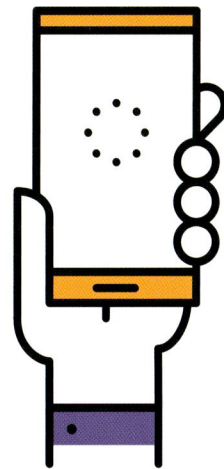

There are lots of weird and wonderful words in the world of social media. This handy guide will help you learn them all – but first, let's take a look at how to De:Code each word.

BITMOJI
(BIT-MO-JEE)
Noun: a customised emoji or avatar that can be added to your social media account. A bitmoji is usually created to look like a virtual version of the account owner. See **AVATAR** and **EMOJI**.

HEADWORD: this shows you how a word is spelt. These words are organised in alphabetical order.

PRONUNCIATION GUIDE: this tells you how to say a word out loud. Say each part exactly how it's written to pronounce the word correctly.

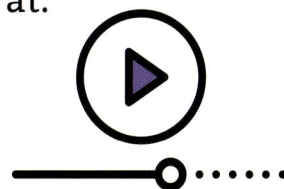

Word class: this is the type of word that the headword is. In this book you will see some of these:
- Noun – a person, place or thing
- Verb – an action word
- Adjective – a describing word

Abbreviations: this is the type of word that the headword is. In this book you will see some of these:
- Initialism – a set of letters taken from several words that are read as individual letters
- Acronym – a set of letters taken from several words that make a new word

Definition: this is what the headword means.

RELATED WORDS: this shows you other words that link to the one you're looking at.

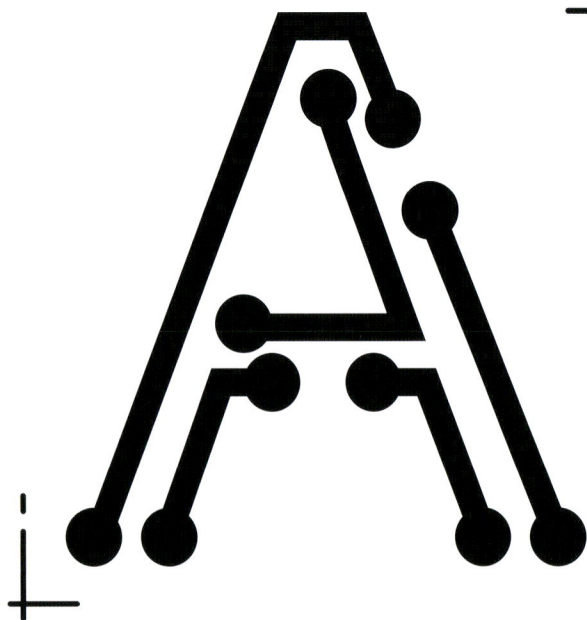

A

AMA (Ask Me Anything)

Initialism: a prompt to other social media users to ask the user anything they want to.

APP

Noun: short for application. An app is a program installed and used on a computer system or portable device. Types of app include games, internet browsers and social media sites.

ACCOUNT

Noun: an online profile that is accessed by one person, or a group of people, to post things to a social media platform. See **PLATFORM**.

ADULTING

Verb: doing things that are very adult or grown-up, such as buying cleaning products or going to work.

AUTHENTICITY (ORTH-EN-TIH-CITY)

Noun: how real a social media account is. If you don't think an account looks like a real person has made it, you should probably stay away from it. See **PHISHING**.

ADVERTISING

Noun: a way that businesses show off their products or services. This can be in the form of videos or images.

Ads.

AVATAR (AH-VUH-TAR)

Noun: an image that represents a person online, usually in forums and on social networks.

B

BAE (Before Anyone Else)
(BAY)
Acronym: a name given to a person by someone that considers them a very close friend.

BAN
Noun: a period of time that a user is not allowed access to their account. A website might give a ban out to a user that has been behaving in a bad way online. This can be thought of as a time-out.

BINGE-WATCHING
Verb: watching lots of videos or TV episodes in a row for very long periods of time without stopping.

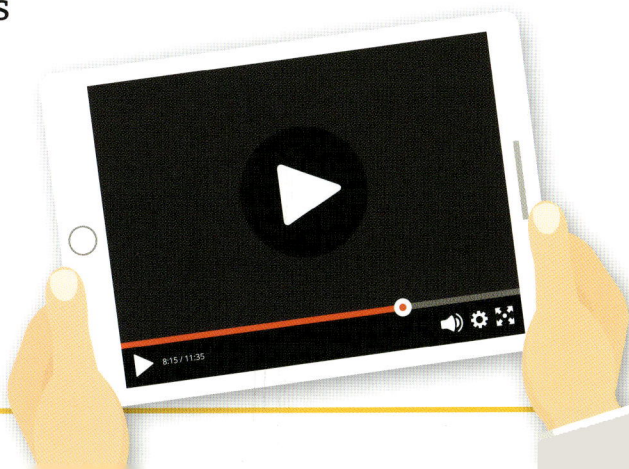

BIO
(BYE-OH)
Noun: short for biography. A bio is a short piece of text on a social media account that the user writes to tell people about themselves. See **ACCOUNT**.

BITMOJI
(BIT-MOH-JEE)
Noun: a customised emoji or avatar that can be added to your social media account. A bitmoji is usually created to look like a virtual version of the account owner. See AVATAR and EMOJI.

BLOCK
Verb: to stop another user from contacting you, seeing your account or tagging you in things. This is a useful feature to keep unwanted accounts from interacting with you.

#ABCDEFGHIJKLMNOPQRSTUVWXYZ

ABCDEFGHIJKLMNOPQRSTUVWXYZ

BLOG

Noun: a website on which a blogger uploads regular pieces of content about a topic.

DID YOU KNOW?

BLOG is a word that was created from two others: 'web' and 'log'. Putting two words together like this is called a blend.

BOOKMARKING

Verb: saving something you found important, enjoyed, or want to continue reading later.

BOOMERANG

Noun: a GIF that plays a very short piece of video and then rewinds it, over and over again. See **GIF**.

BOT

Noun: a program that is made to behave like a real person online and can interact with a system user.

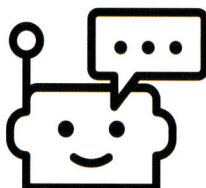

BRB (Be Right Back)

Initialism: a phrase used to let others know you'll be taking a short break. This could be useful should you need to take a secret trip to the toilet.

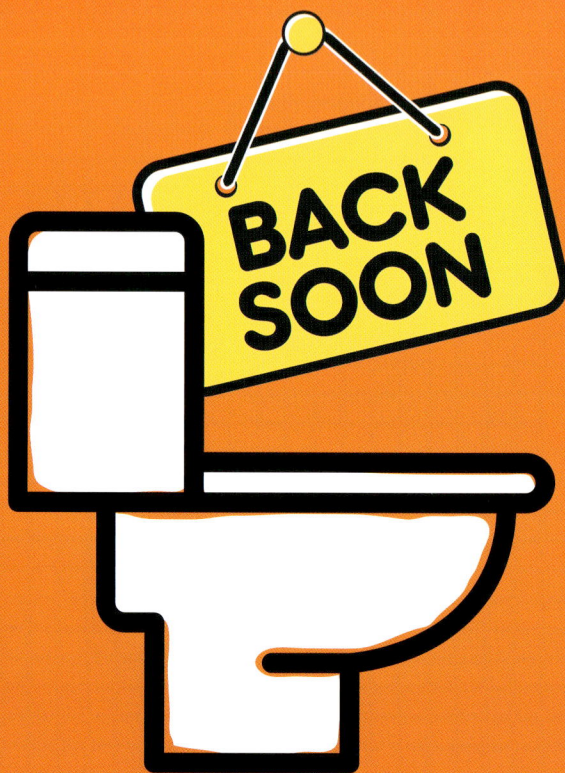

BACK SOON

CHATBOT

Noun: a type of bot that can be found in a messaging app and uses prompts to simulate a conversation. Lots of companies use these to talk to customers if they don't have enough employees available. See **BOT**.

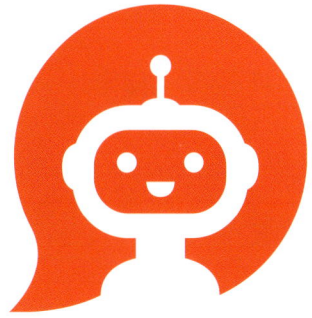

CHECK IN

Verb: to post where you are on social media. This could be to let people know you're visiting somewhere super-cool!

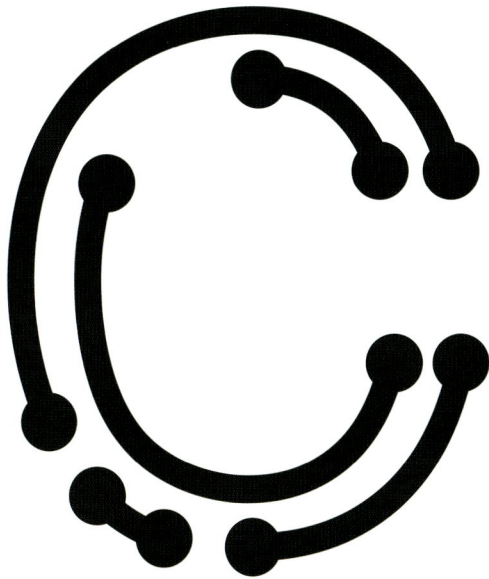

CAPTION (CAP-SHUN)

Noun: a small description that appears below a photo post.

CHARACTER

Noun: one letter, symbol, space or punctuation mark used in some text. For example, a single tweet can be a maximum of 240 characters in length. See **TWITTER**.

CLICKBAIT

Noun: a title or advert made to look so interesting that lots of people click on it. The web page it links to usually has very little to do with the title or advert that you clicked on.

YOU WON'T **BELIEVE** THE DEFINITION FOR THIS WORD...

CHAT

Noun: any kind of communication over the internet. This normally refers to a one-to-one conversation through a messaging app. See **APP**.

#ABCDEFGHIJKLMNOPQRSTUVWXYZ

COMMENT

Noun: a response that is often provided as an answer or reaction to a blog post or a post on a social network.

COMMUNICATION TECHNOLOGY

Noun: equipment, such as mobile phones and tablets, that we use to communicate with other people.

CREEP

Verb: to spend an extended period of time looking through someone's social media profile.

CYBERBULLYING

(SIGH-BUR-BULLY-ING)

Verb: doing something cruel on the internet, usually again and again, to make another person feel angry, sad or scared.

If you are being bullied online, here are a few tips on what to do:

- Tell an adult you trust that you're being bullied.

- Don't respond to the messages – this is what the bullies want.

- Block users that send you nasty messages. See **BLOCK**.

- Save any nasty messages you receive and make a note of when you received them, just in case you need to show these to someone at a later date.

- Visit websites such as: https://www.bullying.co.uk/ cyberbullying/, https://www. connectsafely.org/tips-to-help-stop-cyberbullying/ and https:// www.childline.org.uk/get-support/ for advice and support.

WORD JUMBLE

Each group of letters below is a jumbled up word from in this book. Can you rearrange the letters and figure out what each word is? If you're finding it a bit tricky, why not flick through the book to check out some of the words that might be jumbled.

1. IPGHIHNS

2. LFAEPMCA

3. TVAARA

4. TOEESSRNCH

5. SMIRAMENTA

6. LVAIR

7. RMENUASE

8. NMEMOCT

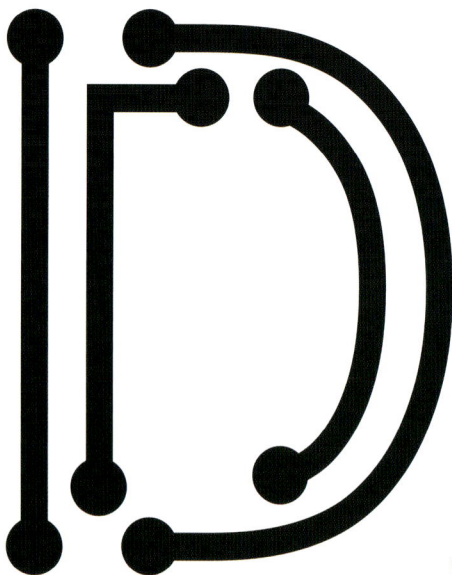

DIGITAL FOOTPRINT

Noun: the information, sometimes personal, left by someone on the internet.

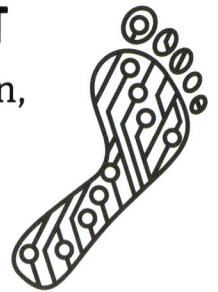

DMs (Direct Messages)

Initialism: a private conversation between two users. Both accounts must usually be following each other to send a message.

DEACTIVATE

Verb: to close a social media account. Sometimes the deleted account can be reopened, and other times it is deleted forever. Always check before you close your account in case you want to reopen it again in the future.

DOWNLOAD

Verb: to copy data from one computer system to another, usually across the internet.

Answers: 1. PHISHING 2. FACEPALM 3. AVATAR 4. SCREENSHOT 5. MAINSTREAM 6. VIRAL 7. USERNAME 8. COMMENT

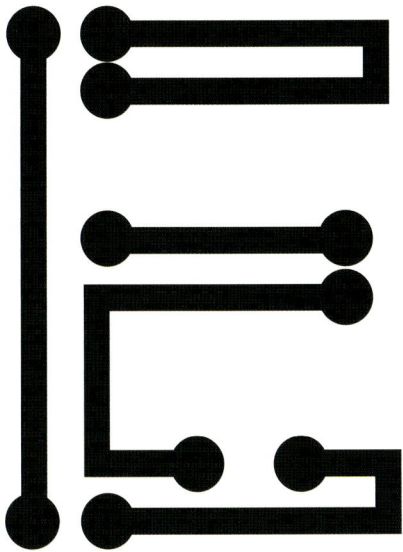

E

DID YOU KNOW?

The first emojis were created and used all the way back in the late 1990s, a long time before the smartphones we know today were invented! They have become so popular that they are now recognised as a digital language, and the Oxford English Dictionary featured 😂 as its word of the year in 2015.

EDIT

Verb: to change something, such as the caption on a photo post. See **CAPTION**.

EMOJI
(EH-MOH-JEE)

Noun: a small icon used to express an idea or an emotion. These are usually used alongside text.

ENGAGEMENT

Noun: the amount that users interact with a particular profile or post. See **POST**.

EXTRA

Adjective: to act very dramatically or over-the-top about something.

A B C D E F G H I J K L M N O P Q R S T U V W X Y Z

FAIL

Verb: an attempt to do something easy that has ended in humiliation for the person trying it. If the fail was REALLY embarrassing, it may even be considered an 'epic fail'.

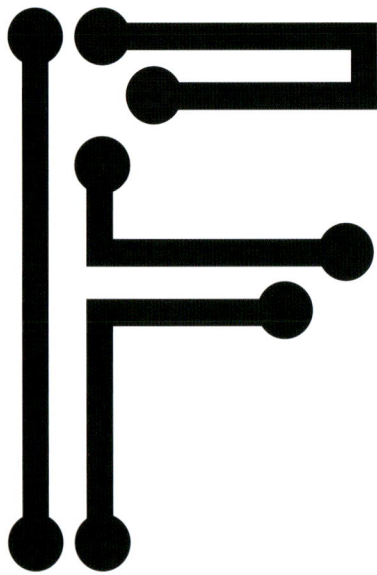

F4F (Follow For Follow)

Initialism: when one user invites others to follow them, with the promise that they will follow them back.

FACEBOOK

Noun: a social media platform founded in 2004, on which you can like, share or comment on people's posts, videos and photos.

FEED

Noun: a list of the latest updates from the accounts that you follow, usually on the social media website's homepage. See **HOME**.

FACEPALM

Verb: when someone says or does something so silly that you can only respond by putting your face into the palm of your hand. This is could be shown in the form of a facepalm emoji or a GIF. See **EMOJI** and **GIF**.

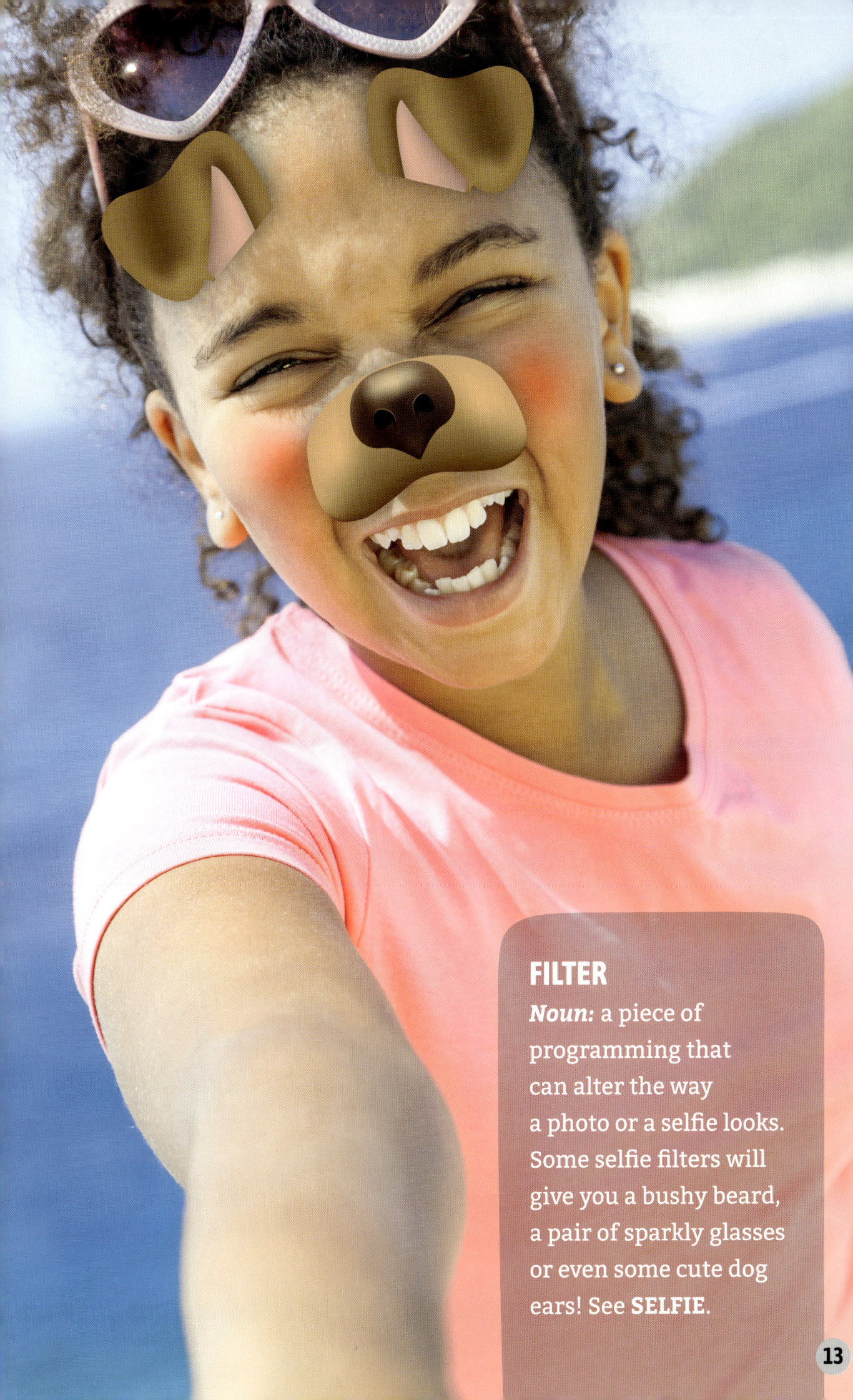

FILTER

Noun: a piece of programming that can alter the way a photo or a selfie looks. Some selfie filters will give you a bushy beard, a pair of sparkly glasses or even some cute dog ears! See **SELFIE**.

FLASH MOB

Noun: a large group of people who gather suddenly in a public place, perform an unusual act, then quickly run away. This is usually filmed and shared on social media.

FOLLOWER

Noun: a person who subscribes to your account in order to receive your updates and posts.

FORUM

Noun: an online discussion site on which people talk about specific topics in a thread. Also known as a message board. See **THREAD**.

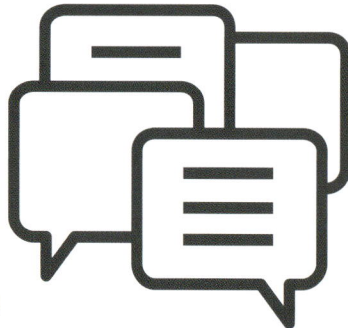

FRENEMY

Noun: someone who you are friendly with but disagree with a lot.

FRIENDS

Noun: the term used on Facebook for the connections you make with people. These are people who you have allowed to connect with you on Facebook, see your profile and interact with you.

G

GOALS
Adjective: something, someone, or some people that others might aspire to be like. For example, #SquadGoals might be used to caption a photo of a group of friends doing something cool or fun.

#SQUADGOALS

GEOTAG
(JEE-OH-TAG)
Noun: a location that can be attached to a social media post to let other people know where you are.

GIF (Graphics Interchange Format)
Acronym: a file that shows a moving image without sound. GIFs rose to popularity on social media because of their likeness to a very short video in an easy-to-use format.

GOAT (Greatest of All Time)
Acronym: a term used to describe someone who is one of the best ever at a particular activity or thing.

GROUP CHAT
Noun: a messaging feature where lots of different users can send messages and everyone can take part in the same conversation.

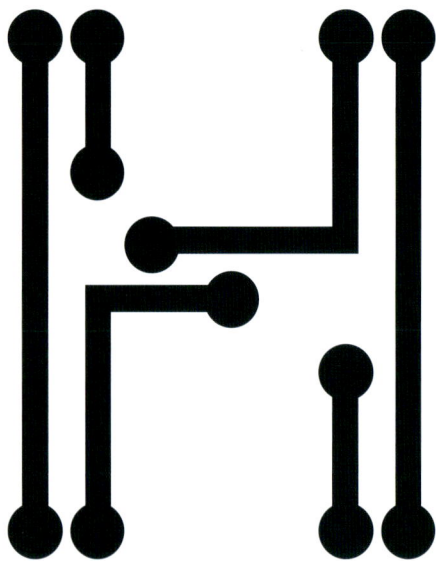

ABCDEFGHIJKLMNOPQRSTUVWXYZ

HANDLE

Noun: someone's @username on Twitter.

HASHTAG

Noun: a tag used on a variety of social networks as a way to annotate a message, using this symbol: #. They usually relate to the topic you're talking about and mean your post can be found in someone's search about that topic. #definition #De:Code #SocialMedia

HIDE

Verb: to make something disappear from your own and other people's feeds, until you stop hiding it. This is useful if you don't want people to see an embarrassing selfie on your page. See **FEED** and **SELFIE.**

HISTORY

Noun: a list of accounts you have viewed or searches that you have made in the past. You can usually clear or delete this.

HOME

Noun: the first page you see when you sign into your social media account.

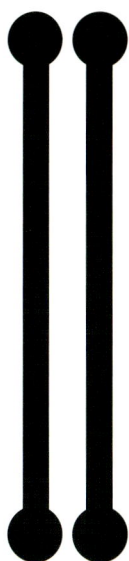

INSTAGRAM

Noun: a photo-sharing app founded in 2010 that lets users take photos, apply filters to their images, and share the photos instantly on the Instagram network.

ICYMI (In Case You Missed It)

Initialism: a signal to point out the latest information or news online that people may not have seen yet.

IMO (In My Opinion)

Initialism: users might write this at the end of a post so that people know it is their personal opinion rather than a fact being posted.

INSTANT MESSAGING

Noun: a type of conversation between two or more people that takes almost no time at all to send messages.

INVITE

Verb: give someone the option of joining a group or a page.

INFLUENCER

Noun: someone who has a large following on social media. This is normally someone who people trust and can be persuaded by because they admire them.

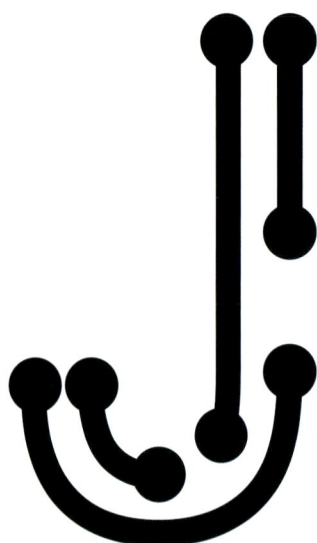

JOIN

Verb: to add yourself to, or become part of, a group or website.

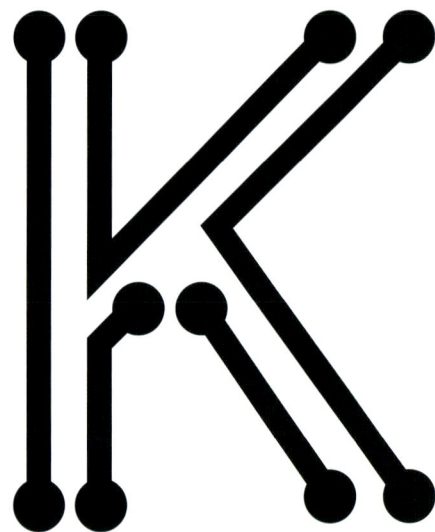

KEEP ME LOGGED IN

Noun: usually a tick box that, if clicked, will stop you from having to enter your details and password every time you enter the website. If you share a computer or device, it might be best to sign in and out every time. See **LOGGING IN/OUT**.

WORD RUSH

There are a lot of words in this book, but how many of them can you make from these letters in just 2 minutes? You can use each letter square just once for each word. Play on your own or grab a friend to challenge. Find a pen, get some paper and start the timer! 3... 2... 1...

C	A	V	R	A	Y
O	U	N	B	M	I
T	E	E	P	K	C
H	A	L	R	V	G
R	D	F	I	E	U
N	Z	G	I	O	M

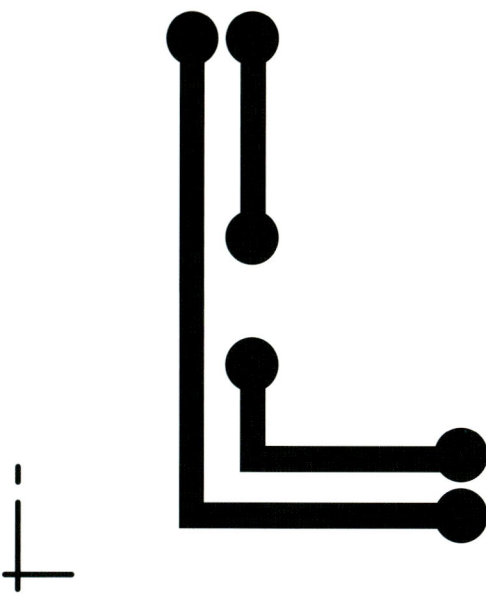

LIVE-POST

Verb: to create posts about an event or situation as it happens.

LOGGING ON/Off

Verb: entering and exiting an account or profile by using your details and a password. Do not leave your accounts logged on while your friends have control of your device. This is a bad idea.

LIKE

Noun: a button that a Facebook, Twitter or Instagram user can press as a quick way to show that they enjoy or support a post.

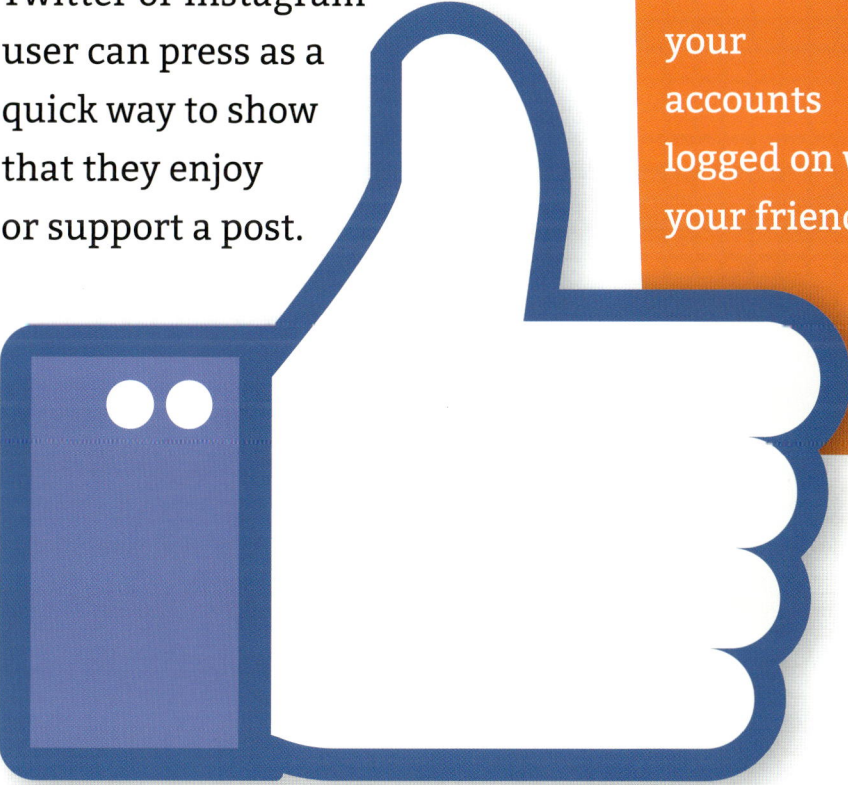

LINK

Verb: to create a virtual bridge from one website to another, in order to direct people somewhere, or to allow information to be shared.

LURKER

Noun: someone who visits and reads forums but doesn't post anything.

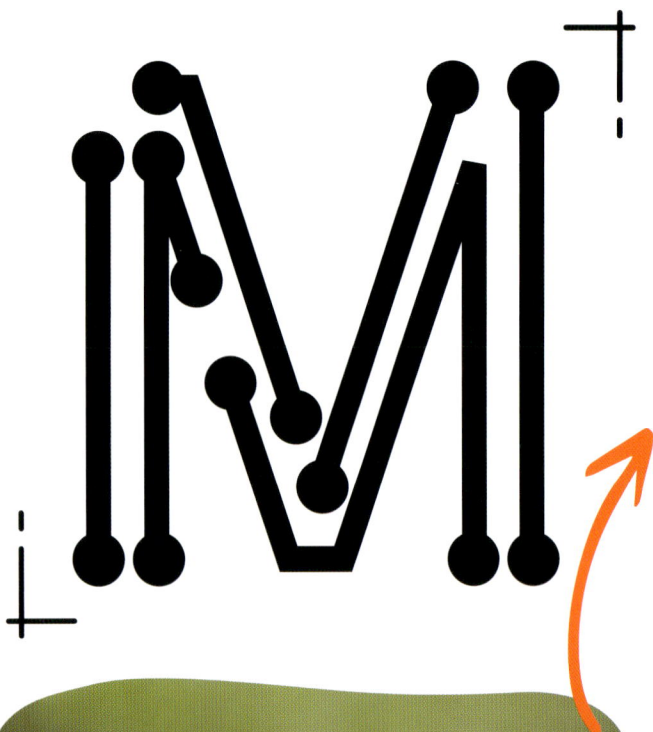

READS DE:CODE

ONCE

MEME (MEEM)

Noun: an image or video, usually with some text, used to describe a thought, idea or joke. They are usually shared online and are intended to make the reader laugh.

MODERATOR

Noun: someone who is in charge of a forum, website or group conversation and has the ability to edit it however they wish. They can also take action against bad or inappropriate behaviour by blocking or removing people. See **BLOCK** and **FORUM**.

MOUSE POTATO

Noun: someone who spends most of their day at a computer.

MUTE

Verb: a way of hiding social media posts from a specific user's account without blocking them. See **BLOCK**.

MUTUAL (MUE-CHOO-ALL)

Adjective: social media users that you follow who also follow you back, or followers or friends that you and another user have in common.

MAINSTREAM

Adjective: something that appeals to most people and becomes popular as a result.

N
P

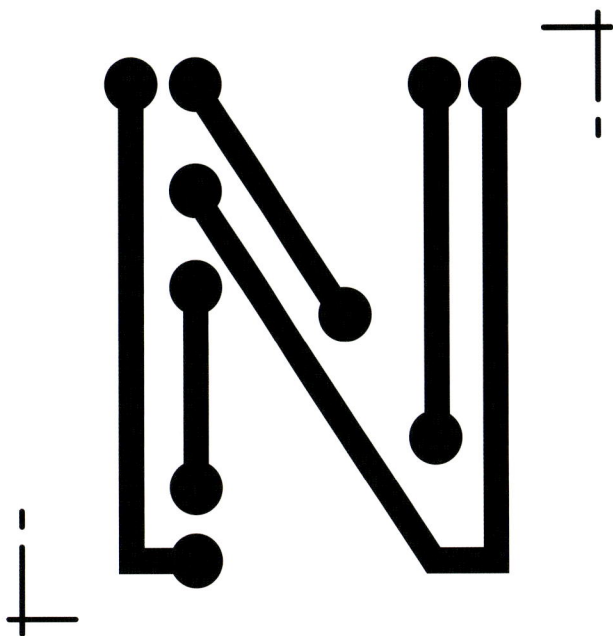

NETIQUETTE
(NET-IH-KET)

Noun: polite behaviour on the internet. For example, typing everything in capital letters is thought to be like shouting, WHICH IS NOT GOOD NETIQUETTE!!!

NETWORK

Noun: a group of users linked together on a social media platform.

NOTIFICATION

Noun: a message or update sharing new social media activity.

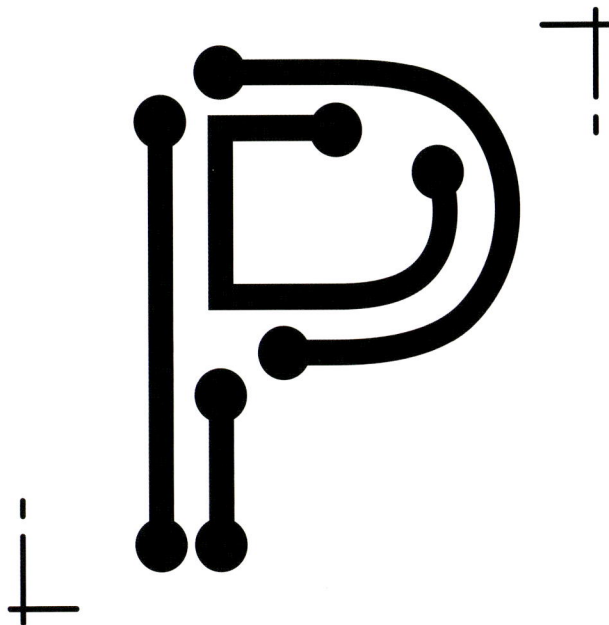

PASSWORD

Noun: a secret combination of letters and numbers (and sometimes other characters) that protects personal information.

How To Choose a Strong Password
- Use at least eight characters
  See **CHARACTER**
- Use upper- and lower-case letters
- Use symbols and numbers
- Don't use easy combinations like '12345678'

PHISHING
(FISH-ING)

Verb: attempting to get personal information such as usernames and passwords over the internet by pretending to be a company or a different person.
See **AUTHENTICITY.**

PHOTOBOMB

Verb: to appear in someone else's photo without them knowing about it, usually ruining the photo or making it funny. These photos sometimes go viral online. See **VIRAL**.

PLATFORM

Noun: a social media website that can be used by anyone with access to the internet.

POST

Noun: a message or form of media, such as a video or photograph, sent to the users who are linked to your account. Your post will appear in their feed. See **FEED**.

PRIVACY

Noun: settings for social media accounts that determine how much of your account can be seen by the public or by your friends or followers. You should change these settings so that your account can't be seen by people you aren't friends with or who don't follow you.

PROFILE

Noun: someone's personal social media page that shows a collection of their posts, information, photos and online activity.

PROMOTED POST

Noun: a post that has appeared on your social media feed from an account you don't follow. This is usually an advertisement paid for by a business.

PUSH NOTIFICATION

Noun: an automatic message sent to your computer, tablet or smartphone by an app, even when the app isn't open. See **APP**.

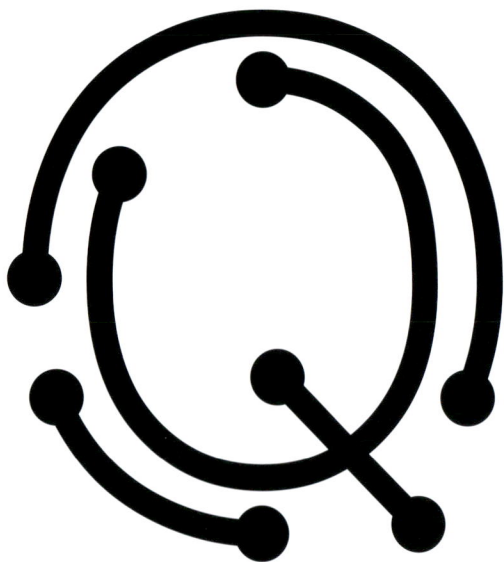

QR CODE

Noun: a square with lots of smaller square and rectangular shapes inside that can be scanned by a device and used to launch a website.

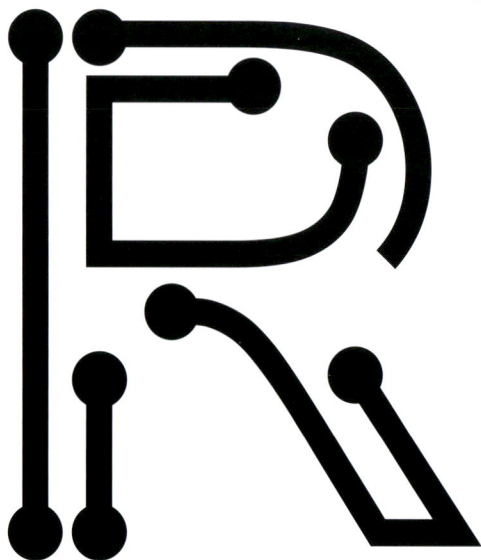

REPLY

Verb: to respond to a direct message or social media post.

REPORT

Verb: to bring a user's behaviour to the website's attention. You might do this if someone is being mean to you online, or has posted something inappropriate.

REQUEST

Noun: an invitation received by someone and sent by someone else for the people to become friends or follow each other on social media. These can be accepted or declined. If you get a request, always make sure you know the user and are happy for them to see your information before you accept it.

RESTRICTED

Adjective: something that is hidden from certain users, usually those under the age of 18.

RETWEET

Verb: when someone on Twitter sees your tweet and decides to share it with their followers. See **TWITTER**.

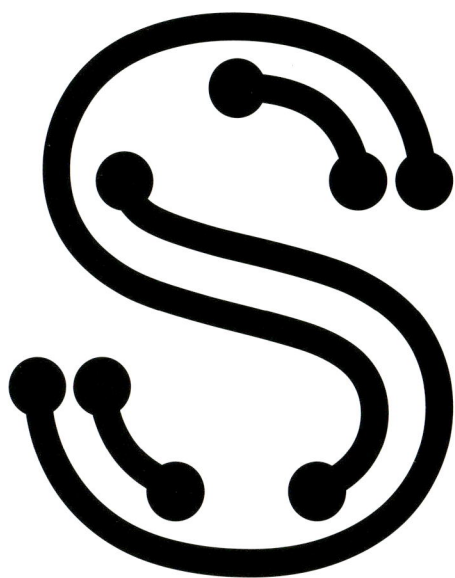

S

SCREENSHOT

Noun: an image taken of whatever is directly on a device's screen.

SEARCH

Verb: using the search bar on a social media platform to find other accounts or posts.

SHARE

Verb: to take a post that you have seen and show it to all the users that follow you.

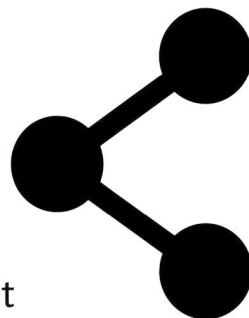

SMH (Shaking My Head)

Initialism: normally used as a reply when someone says something so silly that you don't know what to say. See **REPLY**.

SUBSCRIBER

Noun: someone who has chosen to follow a social media account so that they are updated when the user uploads new content.

SELFIE
(SELL-FEE)

Noun: a photograph that you take of yourself, usually with your smartphone camera.

SNAPCHAT

Noun: an app that allows users to send and receive photos and videos that disappear either straightaway, or after 24 hours.

SOCIAL NETWORK

Noun: a website or app that lets users communicate with each other by creating and sharing posts and messaging each other.

SPAM

Noun: annoying and repetitive social media content that clogs up your feed. Not the popular 20th century meat in a can.

STORY

Noun: a string of photos or videos posted by a social media user that are only visible for 24 hours.

STREAMING

Verb: watching a video file or listening to a music file at almost the same time that it is being downloaded by your computer. This way, you don't have to wait for it to be downloaded first.

Pin Chat Like Feed Follow Mail Call Play SMS Share Search Tag

SPAM
CHOPPED PORK AND HAM

LICENCED BY:
Hormel Foods
Serving Suggestion

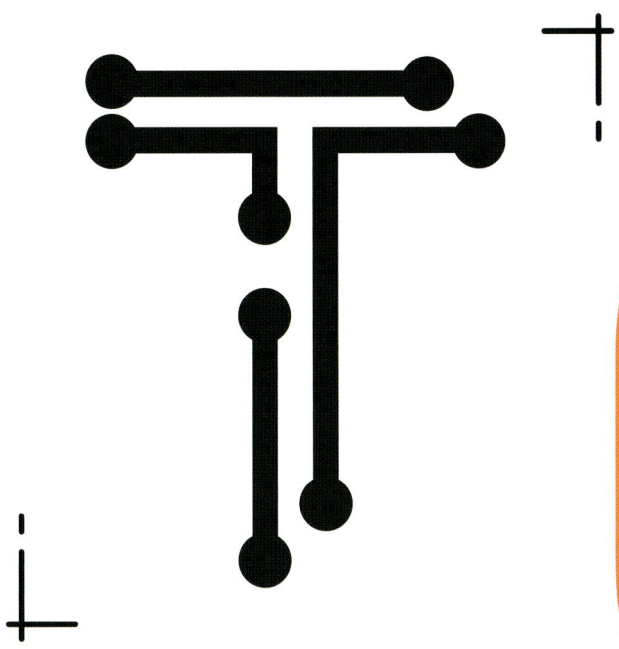

THROWBACK THURSDAY

Noun: also known as '#tbt', social media users post memories for the entertainment of others.

TRENDING

Verb: to be one of the most talked-about topics on a social media platform.

TAG

Verb: to create a link in a comment to another user's account, in order to notify them of a social media post.

TERMS & CONDITIONS

Noun: a set of rules that you must agree to follow before you use a social media platform. If you don't follow these rules, you could be banned from the website!

THREAD

Noun: a series of messages or posts on the same topic on a social media platform. These can represent real-life conversations.

TROLL

Noun: a person who creates controversy on social media. Trolls are known for disrupting conversations online to get angry reactions from other users or to make them feel sad.

TWITTER

Noun: a social media platform founded in 2006, on which users post and interact with 'tweets'.

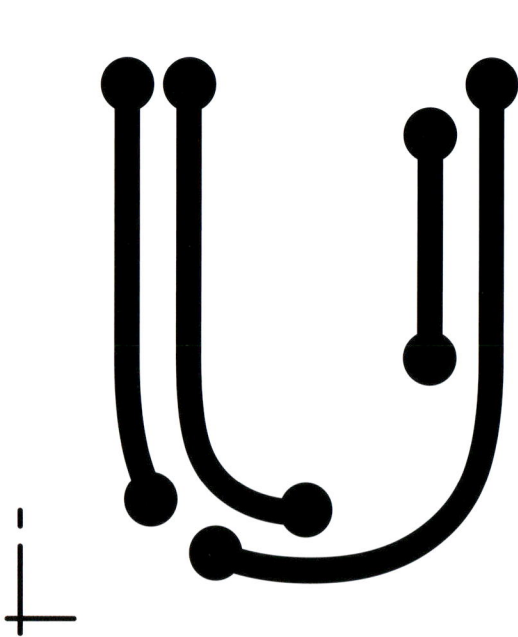

U

UPLOAD

Verb: to post something on the internet. You should always be certain that you want to upload something before you make it visible to the world.

USER-GENERATED CONTENT

Noun: information or media created for social media by the people that use it. This might be in the form of videos, blogs, photos and much more.

UNBOXING VIDEO

Noun: a type of video shared online in which someone opens a new product and unpacks everything in the box to give users an idea of what's inside.

USERNAME

Noun: a name you give yourself to log in to accounts, which you can choose yourself and does not need to be your own name.

UNFOLLOW/UNFRIEND

Verb: remove a user from the list of users that you are linked to. Never be afraid to do this.

CREATE YOUR USERNAME

Are you finding it hard to come up with a cool username for your social media account? Don't worry, this handy generator will make the decision for you! Find the **month of your birthday** and put it together with **the first letter of your name** to find out your username.

January: **Shining**

February: **Crazy**

March: **Selfie**

April: **Awesome**

May: **Scary**

June: **Mainstream**

July: **Viral**

August: **Cartoon**

September: **Verified**

October: **Super**

November: **Sneaky**

December: **YOLO**

A: **Umbrella**

B: **Potato**

C: **Spoon**

D: **Hamster**

E: **Boss**

F: **Hero**

G: **Emoji**

H: **Cloud**

I: **Vampire**

J: **Gravy**

K: **Parsnip**

L: **GOAT**

M: **Genius**

N: **Ghost**

O: **Owl**

P: **Sauce**

Q: **Icon**

R: **Tractor**

S: **Unicorn**

T: **Crown**

U: **Sword**

V: **Bubble**

W: **Legend**

X: **Share**

Y: **Viking**

Z: **Parrot**

👤 Username

🔒 Password   Forgot password?

Sign In

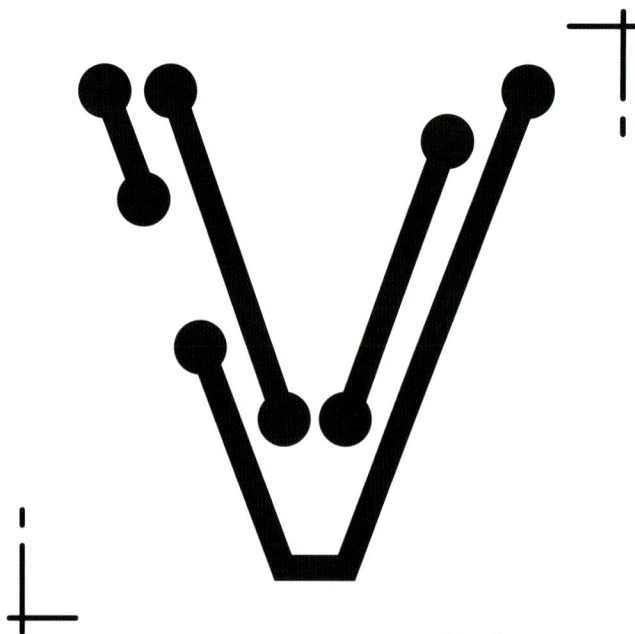

VIRAL

Adjective: content that has spread across social media platforms very quickly by many users interacting with it. Not related to diseases.

Things likely to 'go viral':

- Dogs stuck in unusual places
- Epic fails
- Photobombs
- Memes
- Cats jumping into walls
- Challenges
- Someone doing a silly dance
- Babies doing cute things

VERIFIED

Adjective: an account that has been reviewed by a social media platform to confirm that the owner is exactly who they say they are, usually shown by a tick next to the username. Lots of famous people use this to stop fake accounts from pretending to be them.

VIEWS

Noun: the number of times a post has been seen, or who a post has been seen by.

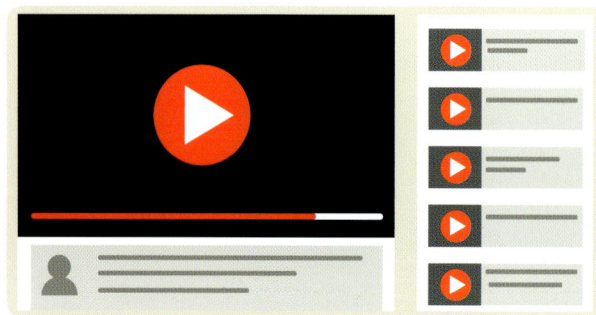

VLOG

Noun: video content created to record the events in someone's life for the entertainment of others. These are normally uploaded to social media websites. The word 'vlog' is created from the words 'video log'.

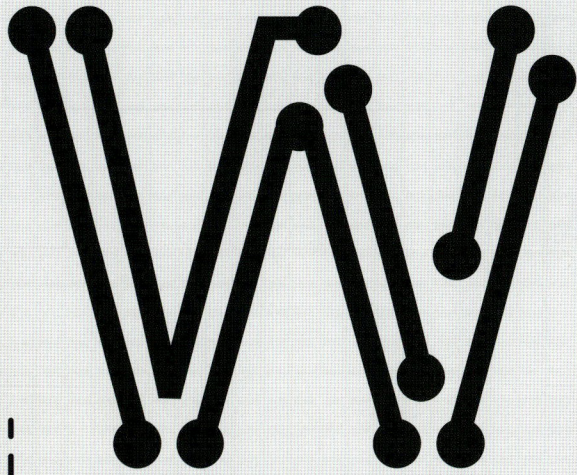

WORLD WIDE WEB

Noun: a collection of web pages found on the internet.

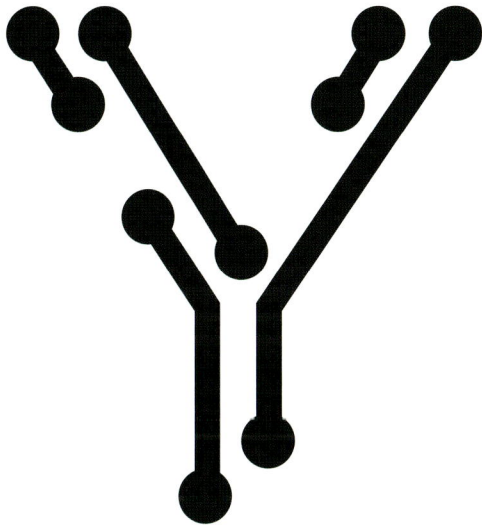

YOLO (You Only Live Once)

Acronym: a phrase you might say or write in a post about doing something silly.

YOUTUBE

Noun: a social media platform founded in 2005, on which users can post videos for their subscribers.

YAAAAAAAS

used when the word 'yes' just isn't enough to express your excitement. Tip: use as many A's as you can.

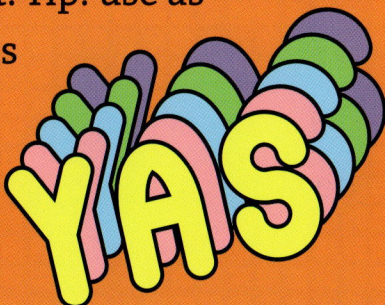

DID YOU KNOW?

YAAAAAAS is an exclamation. This means it's a word that expresses a strong emotion, such as surprise, approval or anger.

WORD SEARCH

You've learned the language of social media, but can you spot some of the words in a crowd? Can you De:Code this word search and find all 15 words?

A	F	I	B	D	W	Y	D	A	R	X	G	O	W	A
G	D	T	E	U	H	F	H	X	E	R	G	J	U	S
K	O	U	L	V	B	F	A	A	P	P	R	W	Q	I
J	W	M	L	H	E	N	S	E	L	F	I	E	U	I
R	N	T	D	T	D	C	H	X	Y	S	Z	A	S	E
H	L	P	P	O	I	U	T	H	J	B	L	O	C	K
G	O	F	R	E	T	N	A	W	M	N	J	Y	T	R
A	A	F	I	S	A	R	G	Y	U	O	P	J	D	C
Q	D	A	V	V	R	Y	B	N	E	M	H	F	G	E
A	F	S	A	T	V	E	R	I	F	I	E	D	E	I
M	J	R	C	V	C	J	U	E	T	H	M	R	O	P
U	S	P	Y	J	F	B	E	X	N	B	Y	S	T	W
T	G	F	A	C	E	P	A	L	M	W	O	M	A	Z
E	H	D	H	U	E	S	V	K	O	A	L	I	G	T
I	P	A	S	S	W	O	R	D	F	D	O	W	C	L

ADULTING
BLOCK
EDIT
GEOTAG
MUTE
PRIVACY
SELFIE
YOLO

APP
DOWNLOAD
FACEPALM
HASHTAG
PASSWORD
REPLY
VERIFIED